Journeying Through the Days 1995

A
Calendar & Journal
for Personal Reflection

Journeying Through the Days 1995

Scripture quotations designated NRSV are from the New Revised Standard Version of the Bible, copyright © 1988 by the Division of Christian Education, National Council of the Churches of Christ in the United States of America. Used by permission.

Scripture quotations designated TEV are from the *Good News Bible*—Old Testament: copyright © American Bible Society 1976; New Testament: Copyright © American Bible Society 1966, 1971, 1976.

Scripture quotations designated NEB are from *The New English Bible* © The Delegates of the Oxford University Press and The Syndics of the Cambridge University Press 1961, 1970. Reprinted with permission.

Scripture quotations designated NIV are from the *Holy Bible: New International Version*. Copyright © 1973, 1978, 1984 International Bible Society. Used by permission of Zondervan Bible Publishers.

Scripture quotations designated KJV are from the King James Version of the Bible.

Scripture selections for each day are chosen from The Revised Common Lectionary copyright 1992 Consultation on Common Texts.

Cover transparency: Frances Dorris
First printing: May, 1994 (18)
ISBN 0-8358-0693-6

Printed in the United States of America

Introduction

Journaling: Breathing Space in the Spiritual Journey

Within the rhythm of our relationship with God, there are times when prayer and meditation seem too ethereal, but the concrete act of gripping a pen seems just right. Forming letters across blank pages provides legible proof that we desire to walk with God. It's as if whatever is churning within us flows through the arm, cascades through the fingers into the pen, and splashes on to the page. There it is for God to see, for us to see. We can then ask God to reorganize all our disorder into peace and purpose. In that quiet space, we develop a conversation with God.

Journeying Through the Days 1995 can provide a quiet breathing space in your spiritual journey. The beautiful color nature photographs, the scriptures for each day, the classic quotations, and the open space to write—all of these work together to lead you into conversation with yourself and with God.

CHRONICLING MORE THAN EVENTS

The spiritual discipline of journaling moves beyond and behind mere descriptions of life events, providing a place to identify and evaluate the pattern our lives are weaving. If a journal answers just one question, it is: What is God doing in my life?

Some of the psalms David wrote seem to have functioned as his journal. When the Philistines had seized David, he described these events in a typical journaling pattern. He began by stating what happened: "Men hotly pursue me" (Psalm 56:1, NIV). He then recorded his feelings: "When I am afraid . . ." (verse 3). He expressed his desires candidly to God: "On no account let them escape" (verse 7). David's hard honesty reveals that journaling is a place to be our true selves and to offer our true, sometimes unflattering, views. We pour out our anguish, think the unthinkable, and presume to know what's best. In the safe haven of being able to make outlandish statements, we stumble across our true motives, feelings, and desires. In a journal, we find the freedom to meander back to God at our own pace. Journal entries may even resemble the conversations between God and Tevya in *Fiddler on the Roof*—sometimes playful, other times ludicrous, still other times heart-wrenching.

In our journals we are free to express the labyrinth of our emotions and desires. David moved from revenge to hopelessness to praise:

> *May the net they hid entangle them,*
> *may they fall into the pit, to their ruin.*
> *O Lord, how long will you look on? . . .*
> *I will give you thanks in the great assembly.*
> (Psalm 35:8, 17, 18, NIV)

This freedom to state such seemingly contradictory feelings soothes our doubts and confusion and provides a resting place for our restless souls. The untidiness of a journal provides a respite from our own or others' expectations of order and appearance. And like meditation, journaling helps us ruminate on truth and weave it into our lives.

HEARING GOD'S VOICE

Sometimes we don't know what to think. How can we journal then? Even though we are taught in school to figure out what we think before writing it, the opposite method sometimes works better. We figure out what we think by first writing it. Writing about our confusion invites God to speak to us and gives us a new way of seeing. This experience is familiar to author Madeleine L'Engle:

> *A help to me in working things out has been to keep an honest, unpublished journal. . . . If I can write things out, I can see them and they are not trapped within my own subjectivity. I have been keeping these notebooks of thoughts and questions and sometimes just garbage (which needs to be dumped somewhere) since I was about nine, and they are, I think, my free psychiatrist's couch.*
>
> *Not long ago someone I love said something which wounded me grievously, and I was desolate that this person could possibly have made such a comment to me.*
>
> *So, in great pain, I crawled to my journal and wrote it all out in a great burst of self-pity. And when I had set it down, when I had it before me, I saw that something I myself had said had called forth the words which had hurt me so. It had, in fact, been my own fault. But I would never have seen it if I had not written it out.*[1]

These Spirit-directed moments of insight occur in journaling partly because of the off-duty mentality journaling encourages. As we pick up the pen, we set aside our evaluations and become simple scribes. We stop living in our minds because we have relinquished our confusion to the page in front of us. That relaxed attitude sets the stage for us to hear God's voice. After writing about what is troubling us, we move on to other topics; but often we begin to understand what we can and cannot do about the dilemma. We see the situation differently.

Journaling does not satisfy all our queries. We may leave our journals filled with unanswered questions—Can we? Will we? When will God . . .? A lack of closure prods us to continue the listening awareness we practiced at the open journal. After days or weeks or months, we are prepared to hear fragments of answers that emerge in the encouragement of a friend or the confrontation of a co-worker. In the meantime, we have learned to rest and listen even though life is full of ferment.

---

[1]Madeleine L'Engle, *Walking on Water* (Wheaton, IL: Harold Shaw Publishers, 1980), p. 137.

RECORDING THE SPIRITUAL JOURNEY

In the spiritual life there are moments that need to be remembered: prayers that are answered incredibly; insights that help us deal with certain kinds of people or situations; goals and dreams that remind us who we are and where we are going; moments when God's grace seems finally to peek through the clouds of our stubbornness; those occasional miracles that no one would believe. John Wesley included one of those moments in his journal. He was reading prayers at Snowsfield when he. . . .

> *saw every thought, as well as action or word, just as it was rising in my heart; and whether it was right before God, or tainted with pride or selfishness. I never knew before . . . what it was "to be still before God."*[2]

I have written such entries after receiving a long awaited promotion, after helping someone in need without telling anyone, after calmly confronting my unruly child. Recording these moments of progress affirms who we are and how God is using us. We do not want to talk *ad nauseam* about them to our friends, but we do need to celebrate these attitudes for which we have fought so hard. God, the only audience for our journal, is no doubt celebrating too.

This conviction that God walks with us makes our journal a safe shelter for confession. Guilt can stir us into overachievement and hyper-productivity. Before we go forth to prove how saintly we are or to refashion friends or spouse into persons they are unwilling to be, we can pause to journal. *What is going on here?* we ask as we feel the drivenness mount. With pen in hand, the confessions pour forth instead of the hyperactivity. "Yes I'm trying to prove to the pastor that I'm the most spiritual person in this church." "Yes, I'm acting like I'm a martyr and my boss is a tyrant." A journal is a place to lay out secrets and be free of their tyranny over us. We state our faults boldly in God's presence and appropriate God's love and acceptance.

The scriptures found in *Journeying Through the Days 1995* offer us another way to respond to God. When we journal after reading scrip-ture, we linger in that scripture for a while and more readily absorb what we have read. We may imagine ourselves as part of the story and assume the identity of one of the characters. We ask ourselves, *How do I feel about Christ? About what he said to me? About what he did?*

Many people record favorite quotations from various books in their journals. Rereading them is as rich as visiting a favorite art museum or eating a piece of cheesecake. The quotations can remind us of our focus. Out of my own journal comes:

---

[2]Paul Lambourne Higgins, ed., *Selections from the Journal of John Wesley* (Nashville, TN: The Upper Room, 1967), p. 11.

Prayer enlarges the heart until it is capable of containing God's gift of himself. Ask and seek, and your heart will grow big enough to receive God as your own.[3]

Establish only one rule: The journal is private. When we write knowing that no one will read our words, we do not worry about grammar or spelling or illegible handwriting. With no audience to impress, we can be completely honest. Many people find it helpful to journal in one special place, such as a favorite chair or a spot in the backyard. Studies suggest that the more special the setting, the better. "Try to find a room where you will not be interrupted or bothered by unwanted sounds, sights, or smells," says psychologist Dr. James Pennebaker.[4]

Although some people journal every day, I journal as needed, which is weekly, bi-weekly, or monthly. I apply the same principle to it that Christ did to the Sabbath: people were not created for their journals; journaling was created for people (see Mark 2:27). Seek God about possible journaling habits. One person's approach may not provide the rest and reflection necessary for another. Whatever the pattern, keep alert for moments that call for journaling. When you feel the urge to confess, to grieve, to rejoice, to surrender, act on it. Pouring this response before God helps you find your center in God. This urge expresses a deeper yearning. Howard Thurman writes:

There is ever present in me a searching longing for some ultimate resting place for my spirit—some final haven of refuge from storms and upheavals of life. I seek ever the kind of peace that can pervade my total life, finding its quiet way into all the hidden crevices of my being and covering me completely with a vast tranquility. This I seek not because I am . . . afraid of living, but because the urge seems to steady me to the very core.[5]

May this journal provide breathing space in the spiritual journey you undertake in this new year.

Jan Johnson

Jan Johnson is a retreat speaker and the author of several books including, When Food Is Your Best Friend (And Worst Enemy) *and* Surrendering Hunger *(HarperSanFrancisco).*

---

[3]Mother Teresa as quoted in Malcolm Muggeridge, *Something Beautiful for God* (San Francisco: Harper & Row, 1986), p. 39.

[4]James Pennebaker, *Opening Up: The Healing Power of Confiding in Others* (New York, NY: Avon Books, 1990), p. 50.

[5]Howard Thurman, *Meditations of the Heart* (New York, NY: Harper & Brothers, 1953), pp. 175-176. Reprinted in 1976 by Friends United Press, Richmond, Indiana.

John Netherton

To walk in the light while darkness invades, envelops, and
surrounds is to wait on the Lord. This is to know the renewal
of strength. This is to walk and faint not.

      Howard Thurman

Sunday, January 1

A loud voice from the throne [said], "See, the home of God is among mortals. He will dwell with them as their God; they will be his peoples, and God himself will be with them; he will wipe every tear from their eyes. Death will be no more; mourning and crying and pain will be no more . . ." (Rev. 21:3-4, NRSV).

Ecclesiastes 3:1-13
Psalm 8
Revelation 21:1-6a
Matthew 25:31-46

Monday, January 2

The Lord said, "Do not fear, for I have redeemed you; I have called you by name, you are mine" (Isa. 43:1*b*, NRSV).

Tuesday, January 3

The LORD will give strength unto his people; the LORD will bless his people with peace (Psalm 29:11, KJV).

Wednesday, January 4

[John] spoke out and said to them all: "I baptize you with water; but there is one to come who is mightier than I" (Luke 3:16, NEB).

Thursday, January 5

The voice of the LORD is heard on the seas; the glorious God thunders, and his voice echoes over the ocean (Psalm 29:3, TEV).

Friday, January 6

EPIPHANY

The Holy Spirit descended on [Jesus] in bodily form like a dove. And a voice came from heaven: "You are my Son, whom I love; with you I am well pleased" (Luke 3:22, NIV).

Saturday, January 7

The Lord said, "When you pass through the waters, I will be with you; and through the rivers, they shall not overwhelm you" (Isa. 43:2a, NRSV).

Jeanene Tiner

It came, a floweret bright,
amid the cold of winter,
when half spent was the night.

    "Lo, How a Rose E'er Blooming"

Sunday, January 8

The voice of the LORD causes the oaks to whirl and strips the forest bare; and in his temple all say, "Glory!" (Psalm 29:9, NRSV).

Isaiah 43:1-7
Psalm 29
Acts 8:14-17
Luke 3:15-17, 21-22

Monday, January 9

Your righteousness is like the mighty
mountains, your justice like the great deep
(Psalm 36:6, NIV).

Tuesday, January 10

There are varieties of gifts, but the same Spirit;
and there are varieties of services, but the same
Lord; and there are varieties of activities, but it
is the same God who activates all of them in
everyone (1 Cor. 12:4-6, NRSV).

Wednesday, January 11

You shall be called by a new name that the mouth of the LORD will give (Isa. 62:2c, NRSV).

Thursday, January 12

Jesus performed this first miracle in Cana in Galilee; there he revealed his glory, and his disciples believed in him (John 2:11, TEV).

Friday, January 13

No one can say, "Jesus is Lord," except by the Holy Spirit (1 Cor. 12:3, NIV).

Saturday, January 14

How precious, O God, is your constant love! We find protection under the shadow of your wings (Psalm 36:7, TEV).

Alan Mills

I still believe that standing up for the truth of God is the greatest
thing in the world. This is the end of life. . . . The end of life is not
to achieve pleasure and avoid pain. The end of life is to do the will
of God, come what may.

Martin Luther King, Jr.

Sunday, January 15

MARTIN LUTHER KING, JR.'S BIRTHDAY

The Spirit gives one person the power to work miracles; to another, the gift of speaking God's message; and to yet another, the ability to tell the difference between gifts that come from the Spirit and those that do not (1 Cor. 12:10*a*, TEV).

Isaiah 62:1-5
Psalm 36:5-10
1 Corinthians 12:1-11
John 2:1-11

Monday, January 16

When the people heard what the Law required,
they were so moved that they began to cry
(Neh. 8:9, TEV).

Tuesday, January 17

This day is sacred to our Lord. Do not grieve,
for the joy of the LORD is your strength (Neh.
8:10, NIV).

Wednesday, January 18

Let the words of my mouth, and the meditation of my heart, be acceptable in thy sight, O LORD, my strength and my redeemer (Psalm 19:14, KJV).

Thursday, January 19

You are the body of Christ, and each one of you is a part of it (1 Cor. 12:27, NIV).

Friday, January 20

The heavens are telling the glory of God; and the firmament proclaims his handiwork (Psalm 19:1, NRSV).

Saturday, January 21

The law of the LORD is perfect; it gives new strength. The commands of the LORD are trustworthy, giving wisdom to those who lack it (Psalm 19:7, TEV).

John Netherton

No writing on the solitary, meditative dimension of life can say anything that has not already been said better by the wind in the pine trees.

Thomas Merton

Sunday, January 22

Jesus read, "The Spirit of the Lord is upon me, because he has anointed me to bring good news to the poor. He has sent me to proclaim release to the captives and recovery of sight to the blind, to let the oppressed go free." Then he began to say to them, "Today this scripture has been fulfilled in your hearing" (Luke 4:18, 21, NRSV).

Nehemiah 8:1-3, 5-6, 8-10
Psalm 19
I Corinthians 12:12-31*a*
Luke 4:14-21

Monday, January 23

Be to me a rock of refuge, a strong fortress, to save me, for you are my rock and my fortress (Psalm 71:3, NRSV).

Tuesday, January 24

The word of the LORD came to [Jeremiah] saying, "Before I formed you in the womb I knew you, and before you were born I consecrated you; I appointed you a prophet to the nations" (Jer. 1:4-5, NRSV).

Wednesday, January 25

If I speak in the tongues of mortals and of angels, but do not have love, I am a noisy gong or a clanging cymbal (1 Cor. 13:1, NRSV).

Thursday, January 26

Paul wrote, "If I have a faith that can move mountains, but have not love, I am nothing" (1 Cor. 13:2*b*, NIV).

Friday, January 27

From birth I have relied on you; you brought
me forth from my mother's womb. I will ever
praise you (Psalm 71:6, NIV).

Saturday, January 28

Love never fails. But where there are
prophecies, they will cease; where there are
tongues, they will be stilled; where there is
knowledge, it will pass away (1 Cor. 13:8, NIV).

Those who attempt to search into the majesty of God will be overwhelmed with its glory.

Thomas à Kempis

Sunday, January 29

[Jesus] said, "Truly I tell you, no prophet is accepted in the prophet's hometown" (Luke 4:24, NRSV).

Jeremiah 1:4-10
Psalm 71:1-6
1 Corinthians 13:1-13
Luke 4:21-30

Monday, January 30

I heard the Lord say, "Whom shall I send? Who will be our messenger?" I answered, "I will go! Send me!" (Isa. 6:8, TEV).

Tuesday, January 31

On the day I called, you answered me, you increased my strength of soul (Psalm 138:3, NRSV).

Wednesday, February 1

Though I walk in the midst of trouble, . . . you stretch out your hand, and your right hand delivers me (Psalm 138:7, NRSV).

Thursday, February 2

The LORD will fulfill his purpose for me; your steadfast love, O LORD, endures forever (Psalm 138:8, NRSV).

Friday, February 3

[Jesus] said to Simon, "Put out into deep water and let down your nets for a catch." Simon answered, "Master, we were hard at work all night and caught nothing at all; but if you say so, I will let down the nets" (Luke 5:4-5, NEB).

Saturday, February 4

Jesus said to Simon, "Do not be afraid; from now on you will be catching people." When they had brought their boats to shore, they left everything and followed him (Luke 5:10b-11, NRSV).

A spiritual life is simply a life in which all that we do comes from the centre, where we are anchored in God: a life soaked through and through by a sense of [God's] reality and claim.

   Evelyn Underhill

Sunday, February 5

Paul wrote, "By the grace of God I am what I am, and his grace to me was not without effect. No, I worked harder than all of them—yet not I, but the grace of God that was with me" (1 Cor. 15:10, NIV).

Isaiah 6:1-8
Psalm 138
1 Corinthians 15:1-11
Luke 5:1-11

Monday, February 6

Cursed are those who . . . make mere flesh
their strength, whose hearts turn away from the
LORD. They shall be like a shrub in the desert,
and shall not see when relief comes (Jer. 17:5-6,
NRSV).

Tuesday, February 7

Blessed are those who trust in the LORD, whose
trust is in the LORD. They shall be like a tree
planted by water, sending out its roots by the
stream (Jer. 17:7-8, NRSV).

Wednesday, February 8

The righteous are guided and protected by the
LORD, but the evil are on the way to their doom
(Psalm 1:6, TEV).

Thursday, February 9

If for this life only we have hoped in Christ, we
are of all people most to be pitied. But in fact
Christ has been raised from the dead, the first
fruits of those who have died (1 Cor. 15:19-20,
NRSV).

Friday, February 10

Happy are those . . . who do not follow the
example of sinners. . . . Instead, they find joy
in obeying the Law of the LORD, and they study
it day and night (Psalm 1:1-2, TEV).

Saturday, February 11

Jesus said, "Woe to you who are rich, for you
have received your consolation. Woe to you
who are full now, for you will be hungry (Luke
6:24-25, NRSV).

Frances Dorris

You never enjoy the world aright, till you see how a sand exhibiteth
the wisdom and power of God.

  Thomas Traherne

Sunday, February 12

Jesus said, "Blessed are you who are poor, for yours is the kingdom of God. Blessed are you who hunger now, for you will be satisfied. Blessed are you who weep now, for you will laugh" (Luke 6:20-21, NIV).

Jeremiah 17:5-10
Psalm 1
1 Corinthians 15:12-20
Luke 6:17-26

Monday, February 13

Do not judge, and you will not be judged. Do
not condemn, and you will not be condemned.
Forgive, and you will be forgiven (Luke 6:37,
NIV).

Tuesday, February 14

VALENTINE'S DAY

When the body is buried, it is mortal; when
raised, it will be immortal. When buried, it is
ugly and weak; when raised, it will be beautiful
and strong (1 Cor. 15:42-43, TEV).

Wednesday, February 15

Just as we have borne the likeness of the earthly man, so shall we bear the likeness of the man from heaven (1 Cor. 15:49, NIV).

Thursday, February 16

Love your enemies, do good to those who hate you, bless those who curse you, pray for those who mistreat you (Luke 6:27-28, NIV).

Friday, February 17

Cease from anger, and forsake wrath: fret not thyself in any wise to do evil (Psalm 37:8, KJV).

Saturday, February 18

If anyone strikes you on the cheek, offer the other also; and from anyone who takes away your coat do not withhold even your shirt (Luke 6:29, NRSV).

Kevin Hogan

Let your heart be empty. Do not fill it with words, with the actions of the mind. Let your heart be wholly empty; then only will it be filled.

J. Krishnamurti

Sunday, February 19

A little while, and the wicked will be no more;
look well, and you will find their place is
empty. But the humble shall possess the land
and enjoy untold prosperity (Psalm 37:10-11,
NEB).

Genesis 45:3-11, 15
Psalm 37:1-11, 39-40
1 Corinthians 15:35-38, 42-50
Luke 6:27-38

Monday, February 20

We, who with unveiled faces all reflect the Lord's glory, are being transformed into his likeness with ever-increasing glory, which comes from the Lord, who is the Spirit (2 Cor. 3:18, NIV).

Tuesday, February 21

A voice came from the cloud, saying, "This is my Son, whom I have chosen; listen to him" (Luke 9:35, NIV).

Wednesday, February 22

Where the Spirit of the Lord is, there is liberty
(2 Cor. 3:17, NEB).

Thursday, February 23

God in his mercy has given us this work to do,
and so we do not become discouraged. We put
aside all secret and shameful deeds; we do not
act with deceit, nor do we falsify the word of
God (2 Cor. 4:1-2a, TEV).

Friday, February 24

When Moses went down from Mount Sinai carrying the Ten Commandments, his face was shining because he had been speaking with the LORD . . . (Exod. 34:29, TEV).

Saturday, February 25

O LORD our God, you answered them; you were a forgiving God to them, but an avenger of their wrongdoings (Psalm 99:8, NRSV).

John Netherton

Let nothing disturb you;
let nothing dismay you;
all things pass:
God never changes.

    Teresa of Avila

Sunday, February 26

Exalt the LORD our God, and worship at his
holy hill; for the LORD our God is holy (Psalm
99:9, KJV).

Exodus 34:29-35
Psalm 99
2 Corinthians 3:12–4:2
Luke 9:28-36

Monday, February 27

The faith that leads to righteousness is in the heart, and the confession that leads to salvation is upon the lips (Rom. 10:10, NEB).

Tuesday, February 28

You . . . shall rejoice in all the good things the LORD your God has given to you and your household (Deut. 26:11, NIV).

Wednesday, March 1

There is no distinction between Jew and Greek;
the same Lord is Lord of all and is generous to
all who call on him (Rom. 10:12, NRSV).

Thursday, March 2

Everyone who calls on the name of the Lord
will be saved (Rom. 10:13, NIV).

Friday, March 3

Jesus answered, "The scripture says, 'Worship the Lord your God and serve only him!'" (Luke 4:8, TEV).

Saturday, March 4

I will say of the LORD, He is my refuge and my fortress: my God; in him will I trust (Psalm 91:2, KJV).

Robert Gantner

I believe that God can and will bring good out of evil, even out of the greatest evil. For that purpose he needs [people] who make the best use of everything.

    Dietrich Bonhoeffer

Sunday, March 5

The Lord said, "Those who love me, I will deliver; I will protect those who know my name. When they call to me, I will answer them; I will be with them in trouble" (Psalm 91:14-15, NRSV).

Deuteronomy 26:1-11
Psalm 91:1-2, 9-16
Romans 10:8b-13
Luke 4:1-13

Monday, March 6

The LORD is my light and my salvation; whom shall I fear? The LORD is the stronghold of my life; of whom shall I be afraid? (Psalm 27:1, NRSV).

Tuesday, March 7

The LORD took [Abram] outside and said, "Look at the sky and try to count the stars; you will have as many descendants as that" (Gen. 15:5, TEV).

Wednesday, March 8

Our citizenship is in heaven, and it is from there that we are expecting a Savior, the Lord Jesus Christ (Phil. 3:20, NRSV).

Thursday, March 9

[The Lord Jesus Christ] will transfigure the body belonging to our humble state, and give it a form like that of his own resplendent body, by the very power which enables him to make all things subject to himself (Phil. 3:21, NEB).

Friday, March 10

One thing I asked of the LORD, that will I seek after: to live in the house of the LORD all the days of my life (Psalm 27:4, NRSV).

Saturday, March 11

Jesus said, "I tell you, you will not see me again until you say, 'Blessed is he who comes in the name of the Lord'" (Luke 13:35, NIV).

Richard L. Gilbert

My Lord is the source of love, I the river's course. Let God's love
flow through me. I will not obstruct it.

Wang Weifan

Sunday, March 12

Jesus said, "Jerusalem, Jerusalem! You kill the prophets, you stone the messengers God has sent you! How many times I wanted to put my arms around all your people, just as a hen gathers her chicks under her wings, but you would not let me!" (Luke 13:34, TEV).

Genesis 15:1-12, 17-18
Psalm 27
Philippians 3:17–4:1
Luke 13:31-35

Monday, March 13

God is faithful, and he will not let you be tested beyond your strength, but with the testing he will also provide a way out so that you may be able to endure it (1 Cor. 10:13*b*, NRSV).

Tuesday, March 14

O God, you are my God, I seek you, my soul thirsts for you; my flesh faints for you, as in a dry and weary land where there is no water (Psalm 63:1, NRSV).

Wednesday, March 15

The Lord said, "As the heavens are higher than the earth, so are my ways higher than your ways and my thoughts than your thoughts" (Isa. 55:9, NEB).

Thursday, March 16

Thus will I bless thee while I live: I will lift up my hands in thy name (Psalm 63:4, KJV).

Friday, March 17

Because you are my help, I sing in the shadow
of your wings. My soul clings to you; your
right hand upholds me (Psalm 63:7-8, NIV).

Saturday, March 18

Because thy lovingkindness is better than life,
my lips shall praise thee (Psalm 63:3, KJV).

Lynn M. Stone

I believe that life is given us so we may grow in love, and I believe that God is in me as the sun is in the color and fragrance of a flower—the Light in my darkness, the Voice in my silence.

Helen Keller

Sunday, March 19

The Lord said, "Come, all you who are thirsty, come to the waters; and you who have no money, come, buy and eat! . . . Listen, listen to me, and eat what is good, and your soul will delight in the richest of fare (Isa. 55:1-2, NIV).

Isaiah 55:1-9
Psalm 63:1-8
1 Corinthians 10:1-13
Luke 13:1-9

Monday, March 20

When anyone is joined to Christ, he is a new being; the old is gone, the new has come (2 Cor. 5:17, TEV).

Tuesday, March 21

In Christ God was reconciling the world to himself, not counting their trespasses against them, and entrusting the message of reconciliation to us (2 Cor. 5:19, NRSV).

Wednesday, March 22

While [the prodigal son] was still a long way off his father saw him, and his heart went out to him. He ran to meet him, flung his arms round him, and kissed him (Luke 15:20, NEB).

Thursday, March 23

The prodigal son's father said, "This son of mine was dead and is alive again; he was lost and is found!" (Luke 15:24, NRSV).

Friday, March 24

We are ambassadors for Christ, since God is making his appeal through us; we entreat you on behalf of Christ, be reconciled to God (2 Cor. 5:20, NRSV).

Saturday, March 25

Blessed is he whose transgressions are forgiven, whose sins are covered (Psalm 32:1, NIV).

To love deeply in one direction makes us more loving in all others.
Anne-Sophie Swetchine

Sunday, March 26

While I kept silence, my body wasted away
through my groaning all day long. Then I
acknowledged my sin to you . . . and you
forgave the guilt of my sin (Psalm 32:3, 5,
NRSV).

Joshua 5:9-12
Psalm 32
2 Corinthians 5:16-21
Luke 15:1-3, 11*b*-32

Monday, March 27

Jesus said, "You always have the poor with you, but you do not always have me (John 12:8, NRSV).

Tuesday, March 28

Those who sow in tears will reap with songs of joy (Psalm 126:5, NIV).

Wednesday, March 29

The Lord said, "I am about to do a new thing; now it springs forth, do you not perceive it? I will make a way in the wilderness and rivers in the desert" (Isa. 43:19, NRSV).

Thursday, March 30

Paul wrote, "I reckon everything as complete loss for the sake of what is so much more valuable, the knowledge of Jesus Christ my Lord" (Phil. 3:8a, TEV).

Friday, March 31

Paul wrote, "I press towards the goal to win the prize which is God's call to the life above, in Christ Jesus (Phil. 3:14, NEB).

Saturday, April 1

The LORD has done great things for us, and we are filled with joy (Psalm 126:3, NIV).

Terry Livingstone

The earth is the Lord's, and the fulness thereof; the world, and they that dwell therein.

Psalm 24:1 (NRSV)

Sunday, April 2

Paul wrote, "I no longer have a righteousness
. . . that is gained by obeying the Law. I now
have the righteousness that is given through
faith in Christ, the righteousness that comes
from God and is based on faith" (Phil. 3:9,
TEV).

Isaiah 43:16–21
Psalm 126
Philippians 3:4–14
John 12:1–8

Monday, April 3

The Sovereign LORD has given me an instructed tongue, to know the word that sustains the weary. He wakens me morning by morning, wakens my ear to listen like one being taught (Isa. 50:4, NIV).

Tuesday, April 4

I trust in you, O LORD; I say, "You are my God." Let your face shine upon your servant; save me in your steadfast love (Psalm 31:14, 16, NRSV).

Wednesday, April 5

[Christ Jesus] emptied himself, taking the form of a slave, being born in human likeness (Phil. 2:7, NRSV).

Thursday, April 6

God . . . highly exalted [Christ Jesus] and gave him the name that is above every name, so that at the name of Jesus every knee should bend . . . (Phil. 2:9-10, NRSV).

Friday, April 7

Behold, the Lord GOD will help me; who is he
that shall condemn me? (Isa. 50:9*a*, KJV).

Saturday, April 8

Jesus said, "Who is greater, the one who is at the
table or the one who serves? Is it not the one
who is at the table? But I am among you as one
who serves (Luke 22:27, NIV).

Whatever our doubts about ourselves and our abilities, God believes in us and can use us in ways far beyond our imagining.

Adrienne and John Carr

Sunday, April 9

"Father," [Jesus] said, "if you will, take this cup of suffering away from me. Not my will, however, but your will be done" (Luke 22:42, TEV).

Isaiah 50:4–9*a*
Psalm 31:9-16
Philippians 2:5-11
Luke 22:14–23:56

Monday, April 10

This is the day on which the LORD has acted: let us exult and rejoice in it (Psalm 118:24, NEB).

Tuesday, April 11

Peter said, "I truly understand that God shows no partiality" (Acts 10:34, NRSV).

Wednesday, April 12

In every nation anyone who fears [God] and does what is right is acceptable to him (Acts 10:35, NRSV).

Thursday, April 13

MAUNDY THURSDAY

As in Adam all die, so in Christ all will be made alive (1 Cor. 15:22, NIV).

Friday, April 14

GOOD FRIDAY

The stone that the builders rejected has become the chief cornerstone. This is the LORD's doing; it is marvelous in our eyes (Psalm 118:22-23, NRSV).

Saturday, April 15

The Lord said, "Be glad and rejoice forever in what I will create, for I will create Jerusalem to be a delight and its people a joy" (Isa. 65:18, NIV).

The great Easter truth is not that we are to live newly after death, but that we are to be new here and now by the power of the resurrection.

    Phillips Brooks

Sunday, April 16

The truth is that Christ has been raised from
death, as the guarantee that those who sleep in
death will also be raised (1 Cor. 15:20, TEV).

Acts 10:34-43
Isaiah 65:17-25
Psalm 118:1-2, 14-24
1 Corinthians 15:19-26
John 20:1-18

Monday, April 17

The God of our ancestors raised Jesus from death . . . to give the people of Israel the opportunity to repent and have their sins forgiven (Acts 5:30-31, TEV).

Tuesday, April 18

Jesus said to [the disciples] again, "Peace be with you. As the Father has sent me, so I send you" (John 20:21, NRSV).

Wednesday, April 19

Let everything that has breath praise the LORD
(Psalm 150:6, NIV).

Thursday, April 20

[Jesus] breathed on [the disciples] and said,
"Receive the Holy Spirit. If you forgive
people's sins, they are forgiven; if you do not
forgive them, they are not forgiven" (John
20:22-23, TEV).

Friday, April 21

To him who loves us and has freed us from our sins by his blood, and has made us to be a kingdom and priests to serve his God and Father—to him be glory and power for ever and ever! (Rev. 1:5-6, NIV).

Saturday, April 22

[This book is] written so that you may come to believe that Jesus is the Messiah, the Son of God, and that through believing you may have life in his name (John 20:31, NRSV).

God Almighty first planted a Garden. And indeed it is the purest of
human pleasures.

  Francis Bacon

Sunday, April 23

"I am the Alpha and the Omega," says the Lord
God, who is and who was and who is to come,
the Almighty (Rev. 1:8, NRSV).

Acts 5:27-32
Psalm 150
Revelation 1:4-8
John 20:19-31

Monday, April 24

Weeping may linger for the night, but joy
comes with the morning (Psalm 30:5, NRSV).

Tuesday, April 25

[Countless angels] cried aloud, "Worthy is the
Lamb, the Lamb that was slain, to receive all
power and wealth, wisdom and might, honour
and glory and praise!" (Rev. 5:12, NEB).

Wednesday, April 26

You have turned my mourning into dancing;
you have taken off my sackcloth and clothed me
with joy, so that my soul may praise you and
not be silent (Psalm 30:11–12a, NRSV).

Thursday, April 27

Jesus said to Simon Peter, "Simon son of John,
do you love me more than these?" . . . [Jesus]
said to him, "Feed my lambs" (John 21:15,
NRSV).

Friday, April 28

To him who sits on the throne and to the
Lamb, be praise and honor, glory and might,
forever and ever! (Rev. 5:13, TEV).

Saturday, April 29

I will not be silent; I will sing praise to you.
LORD, you are my God; I will give you thanks
forever (Psalm 30:12, TEV).

Just as a circle embraces all that is within it, so does the God-head
embrace all. No one has the power to divide this circle, to surpass it,
or to limit it.

Hildegarde of Bingen

Sunday, April 30

Jesus said, "I tell you the truth, when you were younger you dressed yourself and went where you wanted; but when you are old you will stretch out your hands, and someone else will dress you and lead you where you do not want to go" (John 21:18, NIV).

Acts 9:1-20
Psalm 30
Revelation 5:11-14
John 21:1-19

Monday, May 1

Jesus said, "The works that I do in my Father's name testify to me" (John 10:25*b*, NRSV).

Tuesday, May 2

Jesus said, "My sheep listen to my voice; I know them, and they follow me. I give them eternal life, and they shall never perish; no one can snatch them out of my hand" (John 10:27-28, NIV).

Wednesday, May 3

The LORD is my shepherd; I shall not want. He maketh me to lie down in green pastures: he leadeth me beside the still waters (Psalm 23:1-2, KJV).

Thursday, May 4

Yea, though I walk through the valley of the shadow of death, I will fear no evil: for thou art with me; thy rod and thy staff they comfort me (Psalm 23:4, KJV).

Friday, May 5

Jesus said, "The Father and I are one" (John 10:30, TEV).

Saturday, May 6

The Lamb, who is in the center of the throne, will be their shepherd, and he will guide them to springs of life-giving water. And God will wipe away every tear from their eyes (Rev. 7:17, TEV).

Frances Dorris

You show me the path of life.
In your presence there is fullness of joy;
in your right hand are pleasures
forevermore.

Psalm 16:11 (NRSV)

Sunday, May 7

Surely goodness and mercy shall follow me all the days of my life, and I shall dwell in the house of the LORD my whole life long (Psalm 23:6, NRSV).

Acts 9:36-43
Psalm 23
Revelation 7:9-17
John 10:22-30

Monday, May 8

Jesus said, "A new commandment I give you: love one another. As I have loved you, so you must love one another" (John 13:34, NIV).

Tuesday, May 9

Jesus said, "If you have love for one another, then everyone will know that you are my disciples" (John 13:35, TEV).

Wednesday, May 10

And he who sat upon the throne said, "I am the Alpha and the Omega, the beginning and the end" (Rev. 21:6, NRSV).

Thursday, May 11

Praise [the Lord], sun and moon; praise him, shining stars. Praise him, highest heavens, and the waters above the sky (Psalm 148:3-4, TEV).

Friday, May 12

John wrote, "I saw a new heaven and a new earth; for the first heaven and the first earth had passed away, and the sea was no more (Rev. 21:1, NRSV).

Saturday, May 13

He who sat on the throne said, "Behold! I am making all things new!" (Rev. 21:5, NEB).

What comes from the heart speaks to the heart.
    Judy Collins

Sunday, May 14

MOTHER'S DAY

Let [everyone] praise the name of the LORD, for
his name alone is exalted; his glory is above
earth and heaven (Psalm 148:13, NRSV).

Acts 11:1-18
Psalm 148
Revelation 21:1-6
John 13:31-35

Monday, May 15

God be gracious to us and bless us, God make his face shine upon us, that his ways may be known on earth and his saving power among all the nations (Psalm 67:1-2, NEB).

Tuesday, May 16

Jesus replied, "If anyone loves me, he will obey my teaching. My Father will love him, and we will come to him and make our home with him" (John 14:23, NIV).

Wednesday, May 17

Jesus said, "Do not let your hearts be troubled, and do not let them be afraid," John 14:27, NRSV).

Thursday, May 18

May the nations be glad and sing for joy, for you rule the peoples justly and guide the nations of the earth (Psalm 67:4, NIV).

Friday, May 19

The gates of the city [the New Jerusalem] will
stand open all day; they will never be closed,
because there will be no night there (Rev. 21:25,
TEV).

Saturday, May 20

Jesus said, "Peace I leave with you; my peace I
give to you; I do not give to you as the world
gives" (John 14:27, NRSV).

All real living is meeting.
　Martin Buber

Sunday, May 21

Jesus said, "I have told you this while I am still with you. The Helper, the Holy Spirit, whom the Father will send in my name, will teach you everything and make you remember all that I have told you" (John 14:25-26, TEV).

Acts 16:9-15
Psalm 67
Revelation 21:10, 22–22:5
John 14:23-29

Monday, May 22

The jailer asked Paul and Silas, "Sirs, what must I do to be saved?" They answered, "Believe in the Lord Jesus, and you will be saved—you and your family" (Acts 16:30-31, TEV).

Tuesday, May 23

Righteousness and justice are the foundation of [the Lord's] throne (Psalm 97:2b, NRSV).

Wednesday, May 24

Jesus prayed, "My prayer is not for [his disciples] alone. I pray also for those who will believe in me through their message" (John 17:20, NIV).

Thursday, May 25

Rejoice in the LORD, O you righteous, and give thanks to his holy name! (Psalm 97:12, NRSV).

Friday, May 26

Jesus prayed, "I have made you known to [his disciples] and will continue to make you known in order that the love you have for me may be in them and that I myself may be in them" (John 17:26, NIV).

Saturday, May 27

The LORD loves those who hate evil; he keeps his loyal servants safe and rescues them from the wicked (Psalm 97:10, NEB).

Roger M. Smith/Vision Impact Photography

God is in every place: suppose it therefore to be a church.
    Jeremy Taylor

Sunday, May 28

He who gives his testimony to all this says,
"Yes indeed! I am coming soon!" So be it.
Come, Lord Jesus! (Rev. 22:20, TEV).

Acts 16:16-34
Psalm 97
Revelation 22:12-14, 16-17, 20-21
John 17:20-26

Monday, May 29

The Spirit that God has given you does not
make you slaves and cause you to be afraid;
instead, the Spirit makes you God's children,
and by the Spirit's power we cry out to God,
"Father! my Father!" (Rom. 8:15, TEV).

Tuesday, May 30

We are God's heirs and Christ's fellow-heirs, if
we share his sufferings now in order to share his
splendour hereafter (Rom. 8:17, NEB).

Wednesday, May 31

O LORD, how manifold are your works! In wisdom you have made them all; the earth is full of your creatures (Psalm 104:24, NRSV).

Thursday, June 1

Bless thou the LORD, O my soul. Praise ye the LORD (Psalm 104:35*b*, KJV).

Friday, June 2

Jesus said to [Philip], "Have I been with you all
this time, Philip, and you still do not know me?
Whoever has seen me has seen the Father. How
can you say, 'Show us the Father'?" (John 14:9,
NRSV).

Saturday, June 3

Jesus said, "Very truly, I tell you, the one who
believes in me will also do the works that I do
and, in fact, will do greater works than these,
because I am going to the Father" (John 14:12,
NRSV).

Frances Dorris

I lift up my eyes to the hills—
    from where will my help come?
My help comes from the LORD,
    who made heaven and earth.

Psalm 121:1-2 (NRSV)

Sunday, June 4

PENTECOST

When the day of Pentecost had come, they were
all together in one place. And suddenly from
heaven there came a sound like the rush of a
violent wind, and it filled the entire house
where they were sitting (Acts 2:1-2, NRSV).

Acts 2:1-21
Psalm 104:24-34, 35b
Romans 8:14-17
John 14:8-17, 25-27

Monday, June 5

O LORD, our Lord, how majestic is your name in all the earth! (Psalm 8:1, NIV).

Tuesday, June 6

When I look at your heavens, the work of your fingers, . . . what are human beings that you are mindful of them . . . ? Yet you have made them a little lower than God, and crowned them with glory and honor (Psalm 8:3-5, NRSV).

Wednesday, June 7

Since we are justified by faith, we have peace with God through our Lord Jesus Christ (Rom. 5:1, NRSV).

Thursday, June 8

We also boast in our sufferings, knowing that suffering produces endurance, and endurance produces character, and character produces hope, and hope does not disappoint us . . . (Rom. 5:3-5, NRSV).

Friday, June 9

God has poured out his love into our hearts by means of the Holy Spirit, who is God's gift to us (Rom. 5:5, TEV).

Saturday, June 10

Jesus said, "All that belongs to the Father is mine" (John 16:15*a*, NIV).

The world will never starve for want of wonders; but only for want
of wonder.

G. K. Chesterton

Sunday, June 11

TRINITY SUNDAY

Jesus said, "I have much more to say to you, more than you can now bear. But when he, the Spirit of truth, comes, he will guide you into all truth" (John 16:12-13*a*, NIV).

Proverbs 8:1-4, 22-31
Psalm 8
Romans 5:1-5
John 16:12-15

Monday, June 12

We know that a person is justified not by the works of the law but through faith in Jesus Christ . . . (Gal. 2:16, NRSV).

Tuesday, June 13

Paul wrote, "It is no longer I who live, but it is Christ who lives in me" (Gal. 2:20*a*, NRSV).

Wednesday, June 14

Paul wrote, "I refuse to reject the grace of God. But if a person is put right with God through the Law, it means that Christ died for nothing!" (Gal. 2:21, TEV).

Thursday, June 15

My voice shalt thou hear in the morning, O LORD; in the morning will I direct my prayer unto thee, and will look up (Psalm 5:3, KJV).

Friday, June 16

Give ear to my words, O LORD, consider my sighing (Psalm 5:1, NIV).

Saturday, June 17

Jesus said to the woman, "Your faith has saved you; go in peace" (Luke 7:50, NIV).

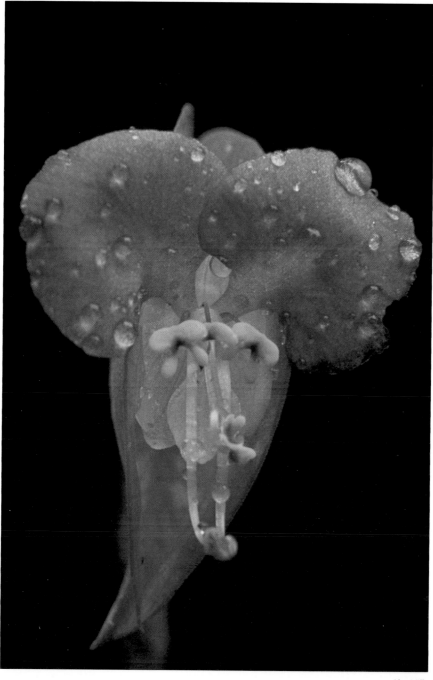

Alan Mills

Beauty is a rare miracle that reduces to silence our doubts about God.

Jean Anouilh

Sunday, June 18

Those who were at the table with [Jesus] began to say among themselves, "Who is this who even forgives sins?" (Luke 7:49, NRSV).

1 Kings 21:1-26a
Psalm 5:1-8
Galatians 2:15-21
Luke 7:36–8:3

Monday, June 19

Jesus said to the Gerasene demoniac, "Return to your home, and declare how much God has done for you" (Luke 8:39a, NRSV).

Tuesday, June 20

As a deer longs for a stream of cool water, so I long for you, O God. I thirst for you, the living God (Psalm 42:1-2a, TEV).

Wednesday, June 21

There is no difference between Jews and Gentiles, between slaves and free men, between men and women; you are all one in union with Christ Jesus (Gal. 3:28, TEV).

Thursday, June 22

If you belong to Christ, then you are Abraham's seed, and heirs according to the promise (Gal. 3:29, NIV).

Friday, June 23

Send forth your light and your truth, let them guide me; let them bring me to your holy mountain, to the place where you dwell (Psalm 43:3, NIV).

Saturday, June 24

Now that faith has come, we are no longer subject to a disciplinarian, for in Christ Jesus you are all children of God through faith (Gal. 3:25-26a, NRSV).

We sing, yet not we, but the Eternal sings in us.
    Thomas R. Kelly

Sunday, June 25

Why are you downcast, O my soul? Why so
disturbed within me? Put your hope in God, for
I will yet praise him, my Savior and my God
(Psalm 42:5, NIV).

1 Kings 19:1-15*a*
Psalm 42 *and* 43
Galatians 3:23-29
Luke 8:26-39

Monday, June 26

Freedom is what we have—Christ has set us
free! Stand, then, as free people, and do not
allow yourselves to become slaves again (Gal.
5:1, TEV).

Tuesday, June 27

You . . . were called to be free. But do not use
your freedom to indulge the sinful nature;
rather, serve one another in love (Gal. 5:13,
NIV).

Wednesday, June 28

The whole law is summed up in a single commandment, "You shall love your neighbor as yourself" (Gal. 5:14, NRSV).

Thursday, June 29

[Our] nature sets its desires against the Spirit, while the Spirit fights against it. They are in conflict with one another, so that what you will to do you cannot do (Gal. 5:17, NEB).

Friday, June 30

I will remember your great deeds, LORD; I will recall the wonders you did in the past. . . . I will meditate on all your mighty acts (Psalm 77:11-12, TEV).

Saturday, July 1

CANADA DAY

Jesus said . . . , "Anyone who starts to plow and then keeps looking back is of no use for the Kingdom of God (Luke 9:62, TEV).

The first thing we are supposed to do is to pay attention.

Diogenes Allen

Sunday, July 2

As [Elijah and Elisha] continued walking and talking, a chariot of fire and horses of fire separated the two of them, and Elijah ascended in a whirlwind into heaven (2 Kings 2:11, NRSV).

2 Kings 2:1-2, 6-14
Psalm 77:1-2, 11-20
Galatians 5:1, 13-25
Luke 9:51-62

Monday, July 3

Bear one another's burdens, and in this way you
will fulfill the law of Christ (Gal. 6:2, NRSV).

Tuesday, July 4

INDEPENDENCE DAY

Do not be deceived; God is not mocked, for
you reap whatever you sow (Gal. 6:7, NRSV).

Wednesday, July 5

Let us not grow weary in doing what is right,
for we will reap at harvest-time, if we do not
give up (Gal. 6:9, NRSV).

Thursday, July 6

As we have opportunity, let us do good to all
people, especially to those who belong to the
family of believers (Gal. 6:10, NIV).

Friday, July 7

You have changed my sadness into a joyful dance; you have taken away my sorrow and surrounded me with joy (Psalm 30:11, TEV).

Saturday, July 8

Jesus said to his disciples, "Whoever listens to you listens to me; whoever rejects you rejects me; and whoever rejects me rejects the one who sent me" (Luke 10:16, TEV).

Frances Dorris

[The desert's] hold on the imagination is the power of subtraction, the abandonment of all names and meanings.

Belden C. Lane

Sunday, July 9

[Jesus] said to them, "The harvest is plentiful,
but the laborers are few; therefore ask the Lord
of the harvest to send out laborers into his
harvest" (Luke 10:2, NRSV).

2 Kings 5:1-14
Psalm 30
Galatians 6:1-16
Luke 10:1-11, 16-20

Monday, July 10

When the true message, the Good News, first came to you, you heard about the hope it offers. So your faith and love are based on what you hope for, which is kept safe for you in heaven (Col. 1:5, TEV).

Tuesday, July 11

All over the world this gospel is producing fruit and growing . . . (Col 1:6, NIV).

Wednesday, July 12

God . . . holds judgment: "How long will you judge unjustly and show partiality to the wicked?" (Psalm 82:1-2, NRSV).

Thursday, July 13

God . . . gives judgment . . .: Defend the cause of the weak and fatherless; maintain the rights of the poor and oppressed (Psalm 82:1, 3, NIV).

Friday, July 14

Paul wrote, "We have not stopped praying for you and asking God to fill you with the knowledge of his will through all spiritual wisdom and understanding" (Col. 1:9, NIV).

Saturday, July 15

[God] hath delivered us from the power of darkness, and hath translated us into the kingdom of his dear Son (Col. 1:13, KJV).

Peggy Darnell

When we are in union with ourselves and with our neighbor, we are one with God.

Gertrud Mueller Nelson

Sunday, July 16

Love the Lord your God with all your heart,
with all your soul, with all your strength, and
with all your mind; and your neighbour as
yourself (Luke 10:27, NEB).

Amos 7:7-17
Psalm 82
Colossians 1:1-14
Luke 10:25-37

Monday, July 17

You must . . . continue faithful on a firm and sure foundation, and must not allow yourselves to be shaken from the hope you gained when you heard the gospel (Col. 1:23*a*, TEV).

Tuesday, July 18

God's plan is to make known his secret . . . for all peoples. And the secret is that Christ is in you, which means that you will share in the glory of God (Col. 1:27, TEV).

Wednesday, July 19

The Lord God says, ". . . Hear this, you that trample on the needy, and bring to ruin the poor of the land, . . . I will turn your feasts into mourning, and all your songs into lamentations" (Amos 8:4, 10, NRSV).

Thursday, July 20

I am like a spreading olive-tree in God's house; for I trust in God's true love for ever and ever (Psalm 52:8, NEB).

Friday, July 21

"Martha, Martha," [Jesus] answered, "you are worried and upset about many things, but only one thing is needed. Mary has chosen what is better, and it will not be taken away from her" (Luke 10:41-42, NIV).

Saturday, July 22

[Christ] himself is before all things, and in him all things hold together (Col. 1:17, NRSV).

The power that makes grass grow, fruit ripen, and guides the bird in flight is in us all.

Anzia Yezierska

Sunday, July 23

[Christ] is the head of the body, the church; he is the beginning, the firstborn from the dead, so that he might come to have first place in everything (Col. 1:18, NRSV).

Amos 8:1-12
Psalm 52
Colossians 1:15-28
Luke 10:38-42

Monday, July 24

Just as you received Christ Jesus as Lord,
continue to live in him, rooted and built up in
him, strengthened in the faith as you were
taught (Col. 2:6-7, NIV).

Tuesday, July 25

When you were baptized, you were buried with
Christ, and in baptism you were also raised
with Christ through your faith in the active
power of God, who raised him from death
(Col. 2:12, TEV).

Wednesday, July 26

[God] has cancelled the bond which pledged us to the decrees of the law. It stood against us, but he has set it aside, nailing it to the cross (Col. 2:14, NEB).

Thursday, July 27

I will listen to what God the LORD will say; he promises peace to his people, his saints—but let them not return to folly (Psalm 85:8, NIV).

Friday, July 28

Steadfast love and faithfulness will meet;
righteousness and peace will kiss each other
(Psalm 85:10, NRSV).

Saturday, July 29

Jesus said, "If you then, though you are evil,
know how to give good gifts to your children,
how much more will your Father in heaven
give the Holy Spirit to those who ask him!"
(Luke 11:13, NIV).

I watch for You, O Holy Spirit, wind that restores life in the overpowering heat of summer. As in the first days, as on Pentecost, You seek here the body which you will make your dwelling-place.

Michel Bouttier

Sunday, July 30

Jesus said, "Ask, and it will be given you; search, and you will find; knock, and the door will be opened. For everyone who asks receives, and everyone who searches finds, and for everyone who knocks, the door will be opened" (Luke 11:9-10, NRSV).

Hosea 1:2-10
Psalm 85
Colossians 2:6-19
Luke 11:1-13

Monday, July 31

You have been raised to life with Christ, so set your hearts on the things that are in heaven, where Christ sits on his throne at the right side of God (Col. 3:1, TEV).

Tuesday, August 1

Take care! Be on your guard against all kinds of greed; for one's life does not consist in the abundance of possessions (Luke 12:15, NRSV).

Wednesday, August 2

Set your minds on things that are above, not on things that are on earth, for you have died, and your life is hidden with Christ in God (Col. 3:2-3, NRSV).

Thursday, August 3

God said, "When Israel was a child, I loved him, and out of Egypt I called my son. But the more I called Israel, the further they went from me" (Hos. 11:1-2*a*, NIV).

Friday, August 4

[You] have clothed yourselves with the new self, which is being renewed in knowledge according to the image of its creator (Col. 3:10, NRSV).

Saturday, August 5

May those who are wise think about these things; may they consider the LORD's constant love (Psalm 107:43, TEV).

Kevin Hogan

I believe a leaf of grass is no less than the journey-work of the stars.
    Walt Whitman

Sunday, August 6

Some wandered in the trackless desert and could not find their way to a city to live in. . . . Then in their trouble they called to the LORD, and he saved them from their distress (Psalm 107:4, 6, TEV).

Hosea 11:1-11
Psalm 107:1-9, 43
Colossians 3:1-11
Luke 12:13-21

Monday, August 7

Faith is the assurance of things hoped for, the conviction of things not seen (Heb. 11:1, NRSV).

Tuesday, August 8

By faith we understand that the universe was formed at God's command, so that what is seen was not made out of what was visible (Heb. 11:3, NIV).

Wednesday, August 9

The Lord said, "Giving thanks is the sacrifice that honors me, and I will surely save all who obey me (Psalm 50:23, TEV).

Thursday, August 10

Where your treasure is, there will your heart be also (Luke 12:34, KJV).

Friday, August 11

What to me is the multitude of your sacrifices? says the LORD; I have had enough of burnt offerings of rams and the fat of fed beasts (Isa. 1:11, NRSV).

Saturday, August 12

It was a better country [Abraham and others] longed for, the heavenly country. And so God is not ashamed for them to call him their God (Heb. 11:16, TEV).

It is a happy world after all. The air, the earth, the water, teem with delighted existence.

William Paley

Sunday, August 13

It was in faith that [Abraham and others] died. They did not receive the things God had promised, but from a long way off they saw them and welcomed them, and admitted openly that they were foreigners and refugees on earth (Heb. 11:13, TEV).

Isaiah 1:1, 10-20
Psalm 50:1-8, 22-23
Hebrews 11:1-3, 8-16
Luke 12:32-40

Monday, August 14

Turn to us, Almighty God! Look down from
heaven at us; come and save your people!
(Psalm 80:14, TEV).

Tuesday, August 15

Jesus said, "Do you think that I have come to
give peace to the earth? No, I tell you, but
rather division! (Luke 12:51, NRSV).

Wednesday, August 16

Since we are surrounded by so great a cloud of witnesses, let us also lay aside every weight and the sin which clings so closely, and let us run with perseverance the race that is set before us (Heb. 12:1, NRSV).

Thursday, August 17

Let us fix our eyes on Jesus, the author and perfecter of our faith, who for the joy set before him endured the cross (Heb. 12:2, NIV).

Friday, August 18

Bring us back, LORD God Almighty. Show us your mercy, and we will be saved (Psalm 80:19, TEV).

Saturday, August 19

Jesus said, "I have a baptism to be baptized with; and how am I straitened till it be accomplished!" (Luke 12:50, KJV).

Roger M. Smith/Vision Impact Photography

We are in love, within love, as fish are in the sea and clouds are in the sky. It surrounds us, penetrates and perfuses us. In a very real sense, we are made of love. Love creates us, and we create love.

Gerald G. May

Sunday, August 20

The vineyard of the LORD of hosts is the house
of Israel, and the people . . . are his pleasant
planting; he expected justice, but saw
bloodshed; righteousness, but heard a cry! (Isa.
5:7, NRSV).

Isaiah 5:1-7
Psalm 80:1-2, 8-19
Hebrews 11:29–12:2
Luke 12:49-56

Monday, August 21

Those who refused to hear the oracle speaking on earth found no escape; still less shall we escape if we refuse to hear the One who speaks from heaven (Heb. 12:25, NEB).

Tuesday, August 22

Jeremiah wrote, "The LORD put out his hand and touched my mouth; and the LORD said to me, 'Now I have put my words in your mouth'" (Jer. 1:9, NRSV).

Wednesday, August 23

The LORD said to [Jeremiah], "Do not say, 'I am only a boy'; for you shall go to all to whom I send you, and you shall speak whatever I command you" (Jer. 1:7, NRSV).

Thursday, August 24

Let us be thankful, then, because we receive a kingdom that cannot be shaken. Let us be grateful and worship God in a way that will please him, with reverence and fear (Heb. 12:28, TEV).

Friday, August 25

You, O LORD, are my hope, my trust, O
LORD, from my youth! (Psalm 71:5, NRSV).

Saturday, August 26

When Jesus saw [the woman who had been
crippled for 18 years], he called her over and
said, "Woman, you are set free from your
ailments" (Luke 13:12, NRSV).

Happiness is not a matter of events; it depends upon the tides of the mind.

　　　Alice Meynell

Sunday, August 27

Jesus answered the synagogue ruler, "You hypocrites! Doesn't each of you on the Sabbath untie his ox or donkey from the stall and lead it out to give it water? Then should not this woman . . . be set free on the Sabbath day from what bound her?" (Luke 13:15-16, NIV).

Jeremiah 1:4-10
Psalm 71:1-6
Hebrews 12:18-29
Luke 13:10-17

Monday, August 28

Do not neglect to show hospitality to strangers, for by doing that some have entertained angels without knowing it (Heb. 13:2, NRSV).

Tuesday, August 29

Remember those who are in prison, as though you were in prison with them. Remember those who are suffering, as though you were suffering as they are (Heb. 13:3, TEV).

Wednesday, August 30

Keep your lives free from the love of money
and be content with what you have, because
God has said, "Never will I leave you; never
will I forsake you" (Heb. 13:5, NIV).

Thursday, August 31

Jesus said to his host, "When you give a lunch or
a dinner, do not invite your friends or your
brothers or your relatives or your rich
neighbors—for they will invite you back, and
in this way you will be paid for what you did"
(Luke 14:12, TEV).

Friday, September 1

When you give a banquet, invite the poor, the crippled, the lame, the blind, and you will be blessed (Luke 14:13-14, NIV).

Saturday, September 2

Do not neglect to do good and to share what you have, for such sacrifices are pleasing to God (Heb. 13:16, NRSV).

It is a difficult lesson to learn today—to leave one's friends and family and deliberately practice the art of solitude for an hour or a day or a week.

Anne Morrow Lindbergh

Sunday, September 3

The Lord said, "Has a nation ever changed its gods? (Yet they are not gods at all.) But my people have exchanged their Glory for worthless idols" (Jer. 2:11, NIV).

Jeremiah 2:4-13
Psalm 81:1, 10-16
Hebrews 13:1-8, 15-16
Luke 14:1, 7-14

Monday, September 4

LABOR DAY

O LORD, you have searched me and known me.
You know when I sit down and when I rise up;
you discern my thoughts from far away (Psalm
139:1-2, NRSV).

Tuesday, September 5

Jesus said, "Whoever comes to me cannot be my
disciple unless he loves me more than he loves
his father and his mother, his wife and his
children, his brothers and his sisters, and
himself as well" (Luke 14:26, TEV).

Wednesday, September 6

I praise you, for I am fearfully and wonderfully
made. Wonderful are your works; that I know
very well (Psalm 139:14, NRSV).

Thursday, September 7

Paul wrote, "I pray that you may be active in
sharing your faith, so that you will have a full
understanding of every good thing we have in
Christ" (Philem. 6, NIV).

Friday, September 8

Whosoever he be of you that forsaketh not all that he hath, he cannot be my disciple (Luke 14:33, KJV).

Saturday, September 9

O God, how difficult I find your thoughts; how many of them there are! If I counted them, they would be more than the grains of sand (Psalm 139:17-18a, TEV).

Terry Livingstone

Beauty and grace are performed whether or not we will or sense
them. The least we can do is try to be there.

Annie Dillard

Sunday, September 10

Can I not do with you, O house of Israel, just as this potter has done? says the LORD. Just like the clay in the potter's hand, so are you in my hand (Jer. 18:6, NRSV).

Jeremiah 18:1-11
Psalm 139:1-6, 13-18
Philemon 1-21
Luke 14:25-33

Monday, September 11

The saying is sure and worthy of full
acceptance, that Christ Jesus came into the
world to save sinners (1 Tim. 1:15, NRSV).

Tuesday, September 12

The LORD looks down from heaven on
humankind to see if there are any who are wise,
who seek after God (Psalm 14:2, NRSV).

Wednesday, September 13

The LORD says, "My people . . . don't know
me. They are like foolish children. . . . They
are experts at doing what is evil, but failures at
doing what is good" (Jer. 4:22, TEV).

Thursday, September 14

Paul wrote, "I give thanks to Christ Jesus our
Lord, who has given me strength for my work.
I thank him for considering me worthy and
appointing me to serve him" (1 Tim. 1:12, TEV).

Friday, September 15

The angels of God rejoice over one sinner who repents (Luke 15:10, TEV).

Saturday, September 16

Joy shall be in heaven over one sinner that repenteth, more than over ninety and nine just persons, which need no repentance (Luke 15:7, KJV).

It is faith that sees miracles.

Frederick Buechner

Sunday, September 17

Jesus told them this parable: "Suppose one of
you has a hundred sheep and loses one of
them—what does he do? He leaves the other
ninety-nine sheep in the pasture and goes
looking for the one that got lost until he finds
it" (Luke 15:3-4, TEV).

Jeremiah 4:11-12, 22-28
Psalm 14
1 Timothy 1:12-17
Luke 15:1-10

Monday, September 18

Jeremiah said, "Since my people are crushed, I
am crushed. . . . Is there no balm in Gilead? Is
there no physician there?" (Jer. 8:21-22*a*, NIV).

Tuesday, September 19

How long, O LORD? Will you be angry
forever? (Psalm 79:5*a*, NIV).

Wednesday, September 20

Whoever is faithful in a very little is faithful also in much; and whoever is dishonest in a very little is dishonest also in much (Luke 16:10, NRSV).

Thursday, September 21

No servant can serve two masters. Either he will hate the one and love the other, or he will be devoted to the one and despise the other. You cannot serve both God and Money (Luke 16:13, NIV).

Friday, September 22

There is one God; there is also one mediator between God and humankind, Christ Jesus, himself human, who gave himself a ransom for all (1 Tim. 2:5-6, NRSV).

Saturday, September 23

Do not remember against us the sins of our ancestors; let your compassion come speedily to meet us, for we are brought very low (Psalm 79:8, NRSV).

Jeff Wiles/Peregrine Photo Art

Faith declares what the senses do not see, but not the contrary of
what they see. It is above them, not contrary to them.

Pascal

Sunday, September 24

Paul wrote, "I urge that petitions, prayers, requests, and thanksgivings be offered to God for all people . . . that we may live a quiet and peaceful life with all reverence toward God" (1 Tim. 2:1-2, TEV).

Jeremiah 8:18–9:1
Psalm 79:1-9
1 Timothy 2:1-7
Luke 16:1-13

Monday, September 25

The love of money is the root of all evil things, and there are some who in reaching for it have wandered from the faith and spiked themselves on many thorny griefs (1 Tim. 6:10, NEB).

Tuesday, September 26

Pursue righteousness, godliness, faith, love, endurance, gentleness (1 Tim. 6:11, NRSV).

Wednesday, September 27

He who dwells in the shelter of the Most High will rest in the shadow of the Almighty (Psalm 91:1, NIV).

Thursday, September 28

[The Lord] will cover you with his feathers and under his wings you will find refuge (Psalm 91:4, NIV).

Friday, September 29

The Lord said, "Because his love is set on me, I will deliver him; I will lift him beyond danger, for he knows me by my name" (Psalm 91:14, NEB).

Saturday, September 30

The Lord said, "When they call to me, I will answer them; I will be with them in trouble, I will rescue them and honor them" (Psalm 91:15, NRSV).

All nature is good.

St. Augustine

Sunday, October 1

Fight the good fight of the faith; take hold of
the eternal life, to which you were called and
for which you made the good confession in the
presence of many witnesses (1 Tim. 6:12, NRSV).

Jeremiah 32:1-3*a*, 6-15
Psalm 91:1-6, 14-16
1 Timothy 6:6-19
Luke 16:19-31

Monday, October 2

God hath not given us the spirit of fear; but of power, and of love, and of a sound mind (2 Tim. 1:7, KJV).

Tuesday, October 3

Do not be ashamed, then, of witnessing for our Lord. . . . Instead, take your part in suffering for the Good News, as God gives you the strength for it (2 Tim. 1:8, TEV).

Wednesday, October 4

Paul wrote, "I am not ashamed, for I know the one in whom I have put my trust, and I am sure that he is able to guard until that day what I have entrusted to him (2 Tim. 1:12, NRSV).

Thursday, October 5

Jesus said to the apostles, "If you had faith the size of a of mustard seed, you could say to this mulberry tree, 'Be uprooted and be planted in the sea,' and it would obey you" (Luke 17:6, NRSV).

Friday, October 6

How can we sing the songs of the LORD while in a foreign land? (Psalm 137:4, NIV).

Saturday, October 7

[God] has saved us and called us to a holy life—not because of anything we have done but because of his own purpose and grace (2 Tim. 1:9, NIV).

Barbara Gasparik

The good news is that God is not only found in sacred places but is
a traveling God.

    Stanley R. Copeland

Sunday, October 8

The servant does not deserve thanks for
obeying orders, does he? It is the same with
you; when you have done all that you have been
told to do, say, "We are ordinary servants; we
have only done our duty" (Luke 17:9-10, TEV).

Lamentations 1:1-6
Psalm 137
2 Timothy 1:1-14
Luke 17:5-10

Monday, October 9

Jesus said, "Were there not ten cleansed? but where are the nine? There are not found that returned to give glory to God, save this stranger" (Luke 17:17-18, KJV).

Tuesday, October 10

Come and see what God has done: he is awesome in his deeds among mortals (Psalm 66:5, NRSV).

Wednesday, October 11

Jesus said to the leper, "Rise and go; your faith
has made you well" (Luke 17:19, NIV).

Thursday, October 12

COLUMBUS DAY

The saying is sure: If we have died with
[Christ], we will also live with him (2 Tim.
2:11, NRSV).

Friday, October 13

Do your best to present yourself to God as one approved by him, a worker who has no need to be ashamed, rightly explaining the word of truth (2 Tim. 2:15, NRSV).

Saturday, October 14

Say to God, "How awesome are your deeds! . . . All the earth bows down to you; . . . they sing praise to your name" (Psalm 66:3-4, NIV).

Grace, which is charity, contains in itself all virtues in a hidden and potential manner, like the leaves and the branches of the oak hidden in the meat of an acorn.

Thomas Merton

Sunday, October 15

Paul wrote, "Remember Jesus Christ, raised
from the dead . . . that is my gospel, for which
I suffer hardship, even to the point of being
chained like a criminal. But the word of God is
not chained" (2 Tim. 2:8-9, NRSV).

Jeremiah 29:1, 4-7
Psalm 66:1-12
2 Timothy 2:8-15
Luke 17:11-19

Monday, October 16

Ever since you were a child, you have known
the Holy Scriptures, which are able to give you
the wisdom that leads to salvation through faith
in Christ Jesus (2 Tim. 3:15, TEV).

Tuesday, October 17

How sweet are thy words unto my taste! Yea,
sweeter than honey to my mouth! (Psalm
119:103, KJV).

Wednesday, October 18

"The time is coming," declares the LORD,
"when I will make a new covenant with the
house of Israel and with the house of Judah"
(Jer. 31:31, NIV).

Thursday, October 19

This is the covenant which I will make . . .,
says the LORD; I will set my law within them
and write it on their hearts; I will become their
God and they shall become my people (Jer.
31:33, NEB).

Friday, October 20

All of [my people], high and low alike, shall know me, says the LORD, for I will forgive their wrongdoing and remember their sin no more (Jer. 31:34, NEB).

Saturday, October 21

When the Son of man comes, will he find faith on earth? (Luke 18:8, NRSV).

One drifting yellow leaf on a windowsill can be a city dweller's fall, pungent and melancholy as any hillside in New England.

E. B. White

Sunday, October 22

All Scripture is inspired by God and is useful for teaching the truth, rebuking error, correcting faults, and giving instruction for right living, so that the person who serves God may be fully qualified and equipped to do every kind of good deed (2 Tim. 3:16-17, TEV).

Jeremiah 31:27-34
Psalm 119:97-104
2 Timothy 3:14–4:5
Luke 18:1-8

Monday, October 23

Paul wrote, "I have done my best in the race, I have run the full distance, and I have kept the faith" (2 Tim. 4:7, TEV).

Tuesday, October 24

Be glad, O people of Zion, rejoice in the LORD your God, for he has given you the autumn rains in righteousness (Joel 2:23, NIV).

Wednesday, October 25

Paul wrote, "The Lord will rescue me from every evil attack and save me for his heavenly kingdom. To him be the glory forever and ever. Amen." (2 Tim. 4:18, NRSV).

Thursday, October 26

Happy are those whom you choose and bring near to live in your courts. We shall be satisfied with the goodness of your house, your holy temple (Psalm 65:4, NRSV).

Friday, October 27

You answer [our prayers] with awesome deeds of righteousness, O God our Savior, the hope of all the ends of the earth and of the farthest seas (Psalm 65:5, NIV).

Saturday, October 28

The grasslands of the desert overflow; the hills are clothed with gladness. The meadows are covered with flocks and the valleys are mantled with grain; they shout for joy and sing (Psalm 65:12-13, NIV).

The fruit of failure may be simply the discovery that we can fail, and survive.

Maria Boulding

Sunday, October 29

The Lord said, "I will pour out my Spirit on all flesh; your sons and your daughters shall prophesy, your old men shall dream dreams, and your young men shall see visions" (Joel 2:28, NRSV).

Joel 2:23-32
Psalm 65
2 Timothy 4:6-8, 16-18
Luke 18:9-14

Monday, October 30

O LORD, how long must I call for help before you listen, before you save us from violence? . . . How can you stand to look on such wrongdoing? (Hab. 1:2-3*b*, TEV).

Tuesday, October 31

HALLOWEEN

O LORD, how long shall I cry for help . . .? The law becomes slack and justice never prevails. The wicked surround the righteous—therefore judgment comes forth perverted (Hab. 1:2, 4, NRSV).

Wednesday, November 1

The LORD answered [Habakkuk] . . .: ". . .
there is still a vision for the appointed time; it
speaks of the end, and does not lie. If it seems to
tarry, wait for it; it will surely come" (Hab.
2:2-3, NRSV).

Thursday, November 2

Thy righteousness is an everlasting
righteousness, and thy law is the truth (Psalm
119:142, KJV).

Friday, November 3

Jesus said to [Zacchaeus], "Salvation has come
to this house today. . . . The Son of Man came
to seek and to save the lost" (Luke 19:9-10,
TEV).

Saturday, November 4

The statutes you have laid down are righteous;
they are fully trustworthy (Psalm 119:138, NIV).

Thomas A. Schneider

O God, in the course of this busy life, give us times of refreshment and peace; and grant that we may so use our leisure to rebuild our bodies and renew our minds, that our spirits may be opened to the goodness of your creation; through Jesus Christ our Lord. *Amen.*

The Book of Common Prayer

Sunday, November 5

Paul wrote, "We always pray for you, asking that our God will make you worthy of his call and will fulfill by his power every good resolve and work of faith" (2 Thess. 1:11, NRSV).

Habakkuk 1:1-4; 2:1-4
Psalm 119:137-144
2 Thessalonians 1:1-4, 11-12
Luke 19:1-10

Monday, November 6

Great is the LORD, and greatly to be praised; his
greatness is unsearchable (Psalm 145:3, NRSV).

Tuesday, November 7

[God] is God not of the dead, but of the living;
for to him, all [of those who have died] are alive
(Luke 20:38, NRSV).

Wednesday, November 8

The LORD is righteous in all his ways and loving toward all he has made (Psalm 145:17, NIV).

Thursday, November 9

Very near is the LORD to those who call to him, who call to him in singleness of heart (Psalm 145:18, NEB).

Friday, November 10

One generation shall praise thy works to another, and shall declare thy mighty acts (Psalm 145:4, KJV).

Saturday, November 11

My mouth will speak in praise of the LORD. Let every creature praise his holy name for ever and ever (Psalm 145:21, NIV).

Terry Livingstone

Humor is a prelude to faith and laughter is the beginning
of prayer.

     Reinhold Niebuhr

Sunday, November 12

May our Lord Jesus Christ himself and God our Father, who loved us and by his grace gave us eternal encouragement and good hope, encourage your hearts and strengthen you in every good deed and word (2 Thess. 2:16-17, NIV).

Haggai 1:15*b*–2:9
Psalm 145:1-5, 17-21
2 Thessalonians 2:1-5, 13-17
Luke 20:27-38

Monday, November 13

Never tire of doing what is right (2 Thess. 3:13, NIV).

Tuesday, November 14

Jesus said, "Watch out; don't be fooled. Many men, claiming to speak for me, will come and say, 'I am he!' and, 'The time has come!' But don't follow them" (Luke 21:8, TEV).

Wednesday, November 15

When you hear of wars and insurrections, do
not be terrified; for these things must take place
first, but the end will not follow immediately
(Luke 21:9, NRSV).

Thursday, November 16

The Lord said, "The wolf and the lamb will feed
together, and the lion will eat straw like the
ox. . . . They will neither harm nor destroy in
all my holy mountain" (Isa. 65:25, NIV).

Friday, November 17

The LORD says, ". . . Be glad and rejoice
forever in what I create" (Isa. 65:17-18, TEV).

Saturday, November 18

It is better to take refuge in the LORD than to
put confidence in mortals (Psalm 118:8, NRSV).

We thank Thee for this place in which we dwell, for the love that unites us, for the peace accorded us this day, for hope with which we expect the morrow, for the health, the work, the food and the bright skies that make our life delightful; for our friends in all parts of the earth.

Robert Louis Stevenson

Sunday, November 19

The Lord said, "Behold, I will create new heavens and a new earth. The former things will not be remembered, nor will they come to mind" (Isa. 65:17, NIV).

Isaiah 65:17-25
Psalm 118
2 Thessalonians 3:6-13
Luke 21:5-19

Monday, November 20

Come and see what the LORD has done. See
what amazing things he has done on earth
(Psalm 46:8, TEV).

Tuesday, November 21

[Christ] is the image of the invisible God, the
firstborn over all creation (Col. 1:15, NIV).

Wednesday, November 22

With joy give thanks to the Father, who has
made you fit to have your share of what God
has reserved for his people in the kingdom of
light (Col. 1:12, TEV).

Thursday, November 23

THANKSGIVING

By the tender mercy of our God, the dawn
from on high will break upon us, to give light
to those who sit in darkness . . ., to guide our
feet into the way of peace (Luke 1:78-79, NRSV).

Friday, November 24

God is our refuge and strength, an ever-present
help in trouble. Therefore we will not fear
(Psalm 46:1, NIV).

Saturday, November 25

[God] has rescued us from the power of
darkness and transferred us into the kingdom of
his beloved Son, in whom we have redemption,
the forgiveness of sins (Col. 1:13-14, NRSV).

Frances Dorris

Were there no God, we would be in this glorious world with
grateful hearts and no one to thank.

    Christina Rossetti

Sunday, November 26

The days are surely coming, says the LORD, when I will raise up for David a righteous branch, and he shall . . . execute justice and righteousness in the land (Jer. 23:5, NRSV).

Jeremiah 23:1-6
Psalm 46; Luke 1:68-79
Colossians 1:11-20
Luke 23:33-43

Monday, November 27

I was glad when they said to me, "Let us go to the house of the LORD!" (Psalm 122:1, NRSV).

Tuesday, November 28

You must always be ready, because the Son of Man will come at an hour when you are not expecting him (Matt. 24:44, TEV).

Wednesday, November 29

You know what time it is, how it is now the moment for you to wake from sleep. For salvation is nearer to us now than when we became believers (Rom. 13:11, NRSV).

Thursday, November 30

The night is far gone, the day is near. Let us then lay aside the works of darkness and put on the armor of light (Rom. 13:12, NRSV).

Friday, December 1

Clothe yourselves with the Lord Jesus Christ,
and do not think about how to gratify the
desires of the sinful nature (Rom. 13:14, NIV).

Saturday, December 2

They shall beat their swords into plowshares,
and their spears into pruning hooks; nation shall
not lift up sword against nation, neither shall
they learn war any more (Isa. 2:4, NRSV).

Barbara Gasparik

There is a correspondence between our hearts and God's. They have imprinted on them the same unimaginable hope, sealed with a promise. Our entire lives are a vigil, a keeping watch, for the fulfillment of this hope.

Wendy M. Wright

Sunday, December 3

In the days to come . . . many peoples shall
come and say, "Come, let us go up to the
mountain of the LORD, . . . that he may teach
us his ways and that we may walk in his paths"
(Isa. 2:2-3, NRSV).

Isaiah 2:1-5
Psalm 122
Romans 13:11-14
Matthew 24:36-44

Monday, December 4

May the God who gives endurance and encouragement give you a spirit of unity among yourselves as you follow Christ Jesus (Rom. 15:5, NIV).

Tuesday, December 5

Receive ye one another, as Christ also received us to the glory of God (Rom. 15:7, KJV).

Wednesday, December 6

John the Baptist came to the desert of Judea and started preaching. "Turn away from your sins," he said, "because the Kingdom of heaven is near!" (Matt. 3:1-2, TEV).

Thursday, December 7

John the Baptist said, "I baptize you with water for repentance, but one who is more powerful than I is coming after me; I am not worthy to carry his sandals. He will baptize you with the Holy Spirit and fire" (Matt. 3:11, NRSV).

Friday, December 8

May the God of hope fill you with all joy and
peace by your faith in him, until, by the power
of the Holy Spirit, you overflow with hope
(Rom. 15:13, NEB).

Saturday, December 9

The wolf shall live with the lamb, the leopard
shall lie down with the kid, . . . and a little
child shall lead them (Isa. 11:6, NRSV).

Frances Dorris

Almighty God, we thank you for making the earth fruitful, so that it might produce what is needed for life: Bless those who work in the fields; give us seasonable weather; and grant that we may all share the fruits of the earth, rejoicing in your goodness; through Jesus Christ our Lord. *Amen*.

The Book of Common Prayer

Sunday, December 10

A new king will arise from among David's descendants. The spirit of the LORD will give him wisdom and the knowledge and skill to rule his people. He will know the LORD's will and have reverence for him, and find pleasure in obeying him (Isa. 11:1-3, TEV).

Isaiah 11:1-10
Psalm 72:1-7, 18-19
Romans 15:4-13
Matthew 3:1-12

Monday, December 11

The LORD feeds the hungry and sets the
prisoner free (Psalm 146:7, NEB).

Tuesday, December 12

Be patient and stand firm, because the Lord's
coming is near (James 5:8, NIV).

Wednesday, December 13

Jesus said, "I assure you that John the Baptist is greater than any man who has ever lived. But he who is least in the Kingdom of heaven is greater than John" (Matt. 11:11, TEV).

Thursday, December 14

Happy is he that hath the God of Jacob for his help, whose hope is in the LORD his God (Psalm 146:5, KJV).

Friday, December 15

The wilderness and the dry land shall be glad,
the desert shall rejoice and blossom; like the
crocus it shall blossom abundantly, and rejoice
with joy and singing (Isa. 35:1-2, NRSV).

Saturday, December 16

Give strength to hands that are tired and to
knees that tremble with weakness. Tell
everyone who is discouraged, "Be strong and
don't be afraid! God is coming to your rescue"
(Isa. 35:3-4, TEV).

To be able to find joy in another's joy, that is the secret of happiness.
George Bernanos

Sunday, December 17

Jesus said to John's disciples, "Go and tell John what you hear and see: the blind receive their sight, the lame walk, the lepers are cleansed, the deaf hear, the dead are raised, and the poor have good news brought to them" (Matt. 11:4-5, NRSV).

Isaiah 35:1-10
Psalm 146:5-10; Luke 1:47-55
James 5:7-10
Matthew 11:2-11

Monday, December 18

Restore us, O God Almighty; make your face
shine upon us, that we may be saved (Psalm
80:7, NIV).

Tuesday, December 19

The Good News was promised long ago by
God through his prophets, as written in the
Holy Scriptures. It is about his Son, our Lord
Jesus Christ: as to his humanity, he was born a
descendant of David (Rom. 1:2-3, TEV).

Wednesday, December 20

The young woman is with child and shall bear a son, and shall name him Immanuel (Isa. 7:14, NRSV).

Thursday, December 21

[Jesus] through the Spirit of holiness was declared with power to be the Son of God by his resurrection from the dead: Jesus Christ our Lord (Rom. 1:4, NIV).

Friday, December 22

An angel said to Joseph, "Do not be afraid to take Mary to be your wife. For it is by the Holy Spirit that she has conceived. She will have a son, and you will name him Jesus—because he will save his people from their sins" (Matt. 1:20-21, TEV).

Saturday, December 23

The people who walked in darkness have seen a great light; those who lived in a land of deep darkness—on them light has shined (Isa. 9:2, NRSV).

The fact of Jesus' coming is the final and unanswerable proof that
God cares.

William Barclay

Sunday, December 24

A child has been born for us, a son given to us;
authority rests upon his shoulders; and he is
named Wonderful Counselor, Mighty God,
Everlasting Father, Prince of Peace (Isa. 9:6,
NRSV).

Isaiah 7:10-16; 9:2-7
Psalm 80:1-7, 17-19
Romans 1:1-7
Matthew 1:18-25

Monday, December 25

Today in the town of David a Savior has been
born to you; he is Christ the Lord (Luke 2:11,
NIV).

Tuesday, December 26

Praise [the Lord], hills and mountains, fruit
trees and forests; all animals tame and wild,
reptiles and birds (Psalm 148:9-10, TEV).

Wednesday, December 27

[Praise the Lord], kings of the earth and all peoples, princes and all rulers of the earth! Young men and women alike, old and young together! (Psalm 148:11-12, NRSV).

Thursday, December 28

The one who sanctifies and those who are sanctified all have one Father. For this reason Jesus is not ashamed to call them brothers and sisters (Heb. 2:11, NRSV).

Friday, December 29

Because he himself was tested by what he suffered, he is able to help those who are being tested (Heb. 2:18, NRSV).

Saturday, December 30

[Joseph] made his home in a town called Nazareth, so that what had been spoken through the prophets might be fulfilled, "He will be called a Nazorean" (Matt. 2:23, NRSV).

Richard L. Gilbert

Never fear shadows. They simply mean there's a light shining somewhere nearby.

Ruth E. Renkel

Sunday, December 31

I will tell of the kindnesses of the LORD, the deeds for which he is to be praised (Isa. 63:7, NIV).

Isaiah 63:7-9
Psalm 148
Hebrews 2:10-18
Matthew 2:13-23; Luke 2:1-20

1995

JANUARY

S	M	T	W	T	F	S
1	2	3	4	5	6	7
8	9	10	11	12	13	14
15	16	17	18	19	20	21
22	23	24	25	26	27	28
29	30	31				

FEBRUARY

S	M	T	W	T	F	S
			1	2	3	4
5	6	7	8	9	10	11
12	13	14	15	16	17	18
19	20	21	22	23	24	25
26	27	28				

MARCH

S	M	T	W	T	F	S
			1	2	3	4
5	6	7	8	9	10	11
12	13	14	15	16	17	18
19	20	21	22	23	24	25
26	27	28	29	30	31	

APRIL

S	M	T	W	T	F	S
						1
2	3	4	5	6	7	8
9	10	11	12	13	14	15
16	17	18	19	20	21	22
23	24	25	26	27	28	29
30						

MAY

S	M	T	W	T	F	S
	1	2	3	4	5	6
7	8	9	10	11	12	13
14	15	16	17	18	19	20
21	22	23	24	25	26	27
28	29	30	31			

JUNE

S	M	T	W	T	F	S
				1	2	3
4	5	6	7	8	9	10
11	12	13	14	15	16	17
18	19	20	21	22	23	24
25	26	27	28	29	30	

JULY

S	M	T	W	T	F	S
						1
2	3	4	5	6	7	8
9	10	11	12	13	14	15
16	17	18	19	20	21	22
23	24	25	26	27	28	29
30	31					

AUGUST

S	M	T	W	T	F	S
		1	2	3	4	5
6	7	8	9	10	11	12
13	14	15	16	17	18	19
20	21	22	23	24	25	26
27	28	29	30	31		

SEPTEMBER

S	M	T	W	T	F	S
					1	2
3	4	5	6	7	8	9
10	11	12	13	14	15	16
17	18	19	20	21	22	23
24	25	26	27	28	29	30

OCTOBER

S	M	T	W	T	F	S
1	2	3	4	5	6	7
8	9	10	11	12	13	14
15	16	17	18	19	20	21
22	23	24	25	26	27	28
29	30	31				

NOVEMBER

S	M	T	W	T	F	S
			1	2	3	4
5	6	7	8	9	10	11
12	13	14	15	16	17	18
19	20	21	22	23	24	25
26	27	28	29	30		

DECEMBER

S	M	T	W	T	F	S
					1	2
3	4	5	6	7	8	9
10	11	12	13	14	15	16
17	18	19	20	21	22	23
24	25	26	27	28	29	30
31						

1996

JANUARY

S	M	T	W	T	F	S
	1	2	3	4	5	6
7	8	9	10	11	12	13
14	15	16	17	18	19	20
21	22	23	24	25	26	27
28	29	30	31			

FEBRUARY

S	M	T	W	T	F	S
				1	2	3
4	5	6	7	8	9	10
11	12	13	14	15	16	17
18	19	20	21	22	23	24
25	26	27	28	29		

MARCH

S	M	T	W	T	F	S
					1	2
3	4	5	6	7	8	9
10	11	12	13	14	15	16
17	18	19	20	21	22	23
24	25	26	27	28	29	30
31						

APRIL

S	M	T	W	T	F	S
	1	2	3	4	5	6
7	8	9	10	11	12	13
14	15	16	17	18	19	20
21	22	23	24	25	26	27
28	29	30				

MAY

S	M	T	W	T	F	S
			1	2	3	4
5	6	7	8	9	10	11
12	13	14	15	16	17	18
19	20	21	22	23	24	25
26	27	28	29	30	31	

JUNE

S	M	T	W	T	F	S
						1
2	3	4	5	6	7	8
9	10	11	12	13	14	15
16	17	18	19	20	21	22
23	24	25	26	27	28	29
30						

JULY

S	M	T	W	T	F	S
	1	2	3	4	5	6
7	8	9	10	11	12	13
14	15	16	17	18	19	20
21	22	23	24	25	26	27
28	29	30	31			

AUGUST

S	M	T	W	T	F	S
				1	2	3
4	5	6	7	8	9	10
11	12	13	14	15	16	17
18	19	20	21	22	23	24
25	26	27	28	29	30	31

SEPTEMBER

S	M	T	W	T	F	S
1	2	3	4	5	6	7
8	9	10	11	12	13	14
15	16	17	18	19	20	21
22	23	24	25	26	27	28
29	30					

OCTOBER

S	M	T	W	T	F	S
		1	2	3	4	5
6	7	8	9	10	11	12
13	14	15	16	17	18	19
20	21	22	23	24	25	26
27	28	29	30	31		

NOVEMBER

S	M	T	W	T	F	S
					1	2
3	4	5	6	7	8	9
10	11	12	13	14	15	16
17	18	19	20	21	22	23
24	25	26	27	28	29	30

DECEMBER

S	M	T	W	T	F	S
1	2	3	4	5	6	7
8	9	10	11	12	13	14
15	16	17	18	19	20	21
22	23	24	25	26	27	28
29	30	31				

1997

JANUARY

S	M	T	W	T	F	S
			1	2	3	4
5	6	7	8	9	10	11
12	13	14	15	16	17	18
19	20	21	22	23	24	25
26	27	28	29	30	31	

FEBRUARY

S	M	T	W	T	F	S
						1
2	3	4	5	6	7	8
9	10	11	12	13	14	15
16	17	18	19	20	21	22
23	24	25	26	27	28	

MARCH

S	M	T	W	T	F	S
						1
2	3	4	5	6	7	8
9	10	11	12	13	14	15
16	17	18	19	20	21	22
23	24	25	26	27	28	29
30	31					

APRIL

S	M	T	W	T	F	S
		1	2	3	4	5
6	7	8	9	10	11	12
13	14	15	16	17	18	19
20	21	22	23	24	25	26
27	28	29	30			

MAY

S	M	T	W	T	F	S
				1	2	3
4	5	6	7	8	9	10
11	12	13	14	15	16	17
18	19	20	21	22	23	24
25	26	27	28	29	30	31

JUNE

S	M	T	W	T	F	S
1	2	3	4	5	6	7
8	9	10	11	12	13	14
15	16	17	18	19	20	21
22	23	24	25	26	27	28
29	30					

JULY

S	M	T	W	T	F	S
		1	2	3	4	5
6	7	8	9	10	11	12
13	14	15	16	17	18	19
20	21	22	23	24	25	26
27	28	29	30	31		

AUGUST

S	M	T	W	T	F	S
					1	2
3	4	5	6	7	8	9
10	11	12	13	14	15	16
17	18	19	20	21	22	23
24	25	26	27	28	29	30
31						

SEPTEMBER

S	M	T	W	T	F	S
	1	2	3	4	5	6
7	8	9	10	11	12	13
14	15	16	17	18	19	20
21	22	23	24	25	26	27
28	29	30				

OCTOBER

S	M	T	W	T	F	S
			1	2	3	4
5	6	7	8	9	10	11
12	13	14	15	16	17	18
19	20	21	22	23	24	25
26	27	28	29	30	31	

NOVEMBER

S	M	T	W	T	F	S
						1
2	3	4	5	6	7	8
9	10	11	12	13	14	15
16	17	18	19	20	21	22
23	24	25	26	27	28	29
30						

DECEMBER

S	M	T	W	T	F	S
	1	2	3	4	5	6
7	8	9	10	11	12	13
14	15	16	17	18	19	20
21	22	23	24	25	26	27
28	29	30	31			